THE BAD DAD JOKE BOOK

HOW MY FATHER RUINED MY CHILDHOOD

(JUST KIDDING!)

By Jack "Pun" Ink

[Written by new dad with a lot of time on his hands while waiting for his son to be born in the hospital at 1AM.]

Breaking News - It's All About The Pun

DISCLAIMER

This eBook is full of fun and silly jokes for adults. Dads, don't share this with your kids, wife, or boss since you are on "company time." But don't take it too seriously! While we have made sure to make this eBook as accurate as possible, we can only guarantee that some of the information here is 100% correct. So have a good time reading it, and don't get mad if some of it doesn't work out for you! If you need more fun, this book isn't for you - so go ahead and ask for your money back!

Now the legal stuff someone probably got sued for not saying in their book somewhere in some long-forgotten court case that set some precedent somewhere in the backwater country...okay...no more rambling.

The information in this eBook is intended to serve as an educational resource. Neither the author nor the publisher can be held liable for errors or omissions that may occur or any resulting losses or damage caused by them. The author and publisher accept no responsibility for any direct or indirect damages that may result from using this eBook.

This eBook provides informative content and should not be used as a substitute for professional medical advice, diagnosis, or treatment. The author and publisher do not guarantee the accuracy of the material provided and bear no responsibility for errors or omissions that may occur. If you require medical advice, please seek assistance from a qualified healthcare provider.

Table of Contents

PROLOGUE

It all began one fateful evening in a living room far, far away. Dad had finished amusing the guests at the dinner party with funny stories and had run out of material to keep them entertained.

Then, a mysterious collection of jokes came from beyond the stars - a beacon of light in the cobwebbed corners of Dad's mind.

He was instantly drawn in by their force field of hilarity and began to read aloud, captivating everyone within earshot with his newfound repertoire of puns and comic strips.

Soon enough, laughter filled the air like ripples on a lake as everyone gathered around to hear Dad's comical tales. And so began an unforgettable journey into the galaxy of dad jokes!

FOREWARD

Hi there! My name is Penelope "LOL" Puns, and I've been married to Jack "Pun" Ink for five years.

You may wonder why I even chose to write the Foreward for this book about terrible non-knee slapping dad jokes, especially since I'm not a fan of them.

But, as much as I may roll my eyes at Jack's jokes now and then, I know how much they mean to him and how much joy they bring to others.

Laughter is the universal language of love, and few things bring more laughter into our lives than dad jokes. They may be silly, cheesy, and often met with groans, but deep down, I know we all secretly love them.

By putting together this book of dad jokes, I've decided to support my husband and his love for puns.

In these pages, you'll find a collection of jokes

that will make you smile, groan, and maybe even laugh out loud.

Whether you're a fan of dry humor, sarcasm, or good old-fashioned puns, there's something in this book for everyone. So, join me on this humorous journey, and let's celebrate the power of laughter and love.

Penelope "LOL" Puns

PS – If this doesn't stop you know from reading and demanding a refund, you're the better man than my husband because he certainly would be *that guy*.

INTRODUCTION

Dads are often the butt of jokes, but dads can also be the funniest people around.

Dads have a reputation for telling terrible jokes, but sometimes they can tell some of the best ones.

Dad jokes are the perfect solution for this problem! They're funny, but not too offensive, and everyone knows what they are so you'll never look like an outsider. Plus, who doesn't love a good dad joke?

Don't be surprised if you find yourself chuckling – this book is filled with snappy dad jokes, puns, and rib-tickling anecdotes from dads everywhere!

Ready for a good time? With an overflowing supply of witty dad jokes and puns, this offers something sure to bring a smile to your face.

Whether you're looking to make the family dinner a bit more fun or want to get some laughs on your next night out, this book is guaranteed to deliver.

So grab your coffee and beer and start enjoying some pun-tastic fun today!

They say that the dad joke dates to the dawn of time.

Legend states that when cavemen and women first invented fire, one father figure proclaimed: "The flame might get a bit too hot at times, but it's sure to bring a spark of laughter to any gathering." And so, the much-loved tradition of dad jokes was born.

Fast forward a few million years, and we're still cracking up over these snappy puns – proving that, once and for all, dad jokes are timeless.

Dad jokes have been around for centuries, but their popularity has grown exponentially in recent years. Dad jokes are beloved by both children and adults alike.

They're a great way to bring cheer and lighten the mood at family gatherings or friendly get-togethers.

And even if you don't find them particularly funny, you can always appreciate a good dad joke's cleverness or creativity.

Dad jokes can be an effective way to break the ice in any conversation. They often get a laugh out of people and express your sense of humor without being too overbearing.

Because dad jokes are usually lighthearted and humorous, they can help to create a more relaxed atmosphere. When used appropriately, dad jokes can help keep the conversation lighthearted and add some laughter.

Using them sparingly is important, as this may make the joke less funny or even annoying for those listening. When using dad jokes in conversation, it's best to use them sparingly and strategically.

Make sure it's funny if you want it to have its desired effect. A good strategy would be to wait for an opportunity in the conversation where you can slip in a clever joke or pun – after all, timing is everything!

Dad jokes have no age limit and can be popular amongst all generations. Whether it's a pun, a witty quip, or a joke with double meanings, dad jokes are sure to bring laughter to any situation.

From grand-dads who tell corny one-liners to fathers who want to make their children giggle, giving out dad jokes is an activity many enjoy.

While some might find the genre of jokes cringeworthy, others appreciate the quick humor and clever wordplay in them.

No matter your opinion of them, there's no denying that dad jokes have been around for some time and remain an entertaining form of comedy.

CHAPTER 1

DEFINITION OF THE "DAD JOKE"

About the only unofficial definition of a "dad joke" I could find came up on UrbanDictionary.com and it was rather inappropriate.

Let's say don't read it if you have sensitive eyes.

So in case your kid ever gets a hold of this dumb book and you don't want your wife to yell at you and ask where did he learn "that word" then here's an all ages version I created for _____ & giggles.

dad joke (däd jōk)

Pronunciation: The sound of "dad" is pronounced like "dawd" and "joke" is pronounced like "johk".

Dad Joke: (noun) A type of joke characterized by its predictable, cheesy humor and often corny delivery.

It is typically told by a father or older male figure and elicits a groan from the listener, rather than a laugh, due to its overly simplistic or obvious punchline.

Bring on the Dad Jokes!

For those old enough to remember, "Dad jokes"

have been around since the early 1990s. When someone tells a "Dad joke," everyone groans and rolls their eyes in unison. But why is it that these jokes are so popular?

Let's look at what makes a Dad joke and why they remain so popular today.

What is a Dad Joke?

A Dad joke is defined as an intentionally corny or cheesy joke, often seen as the kind of joke only a dad would tell. In general, these jokes are usually puns or plays on words that make no real sense.

Think about it - have you ever heard your dad tell a joke and then laugh hysterically afterward?

He was likely the only one laughing because nobody else found it funny. That's exactly what makes up a dad joke: bad puns with no real punchline.

Why Do People Like Them?

This may be hard to believe, but there is an

explanation for why people enjoy bad dad jokes so much.

Believe it or not, scientists have researched this phenomenon and found that most people find humor in these kinds of jokes because they represent nostalgia and familiarity.

They reminded us of our childhood when our dads were telling us these types of jokes all the time - even if we didn't quite understand them then!

So now, when we hear them again, they make us smile and feel nostalgic for those happy times from long ago.

It also helps that these jokes bring out the inner child in all of us by allowing us to playfully tease one another without taking ourselves too seriously – something adults don't get to do very often in life.

As silly as it sounds, this type of joking can even help foster relationships between people who wouldn't otherwise become friends due to age differences or other factors! Who knew?

Dad jokes are here to stay! They may be corny

and cheesy, but they still manage to bring out our inner child and evoke feelings of nostalgia from our childhood days when we first heard our dads telling them to us (and trying not to crack up).

Whether you love or hate them, there's no denying that Dad jokes will always remain popular among generations, young and old alike – even if nobody ever laughs at them!

So don't be afraid to share your favorite dad joke with your friends; you never know how much joy it can bring! #dadjokesforever 😎 😜

CHAPTER 2

THE ORIGIN OF DAD'S JOKES

What Makes A True Dad Joke?

A true dad joke typically includes a pun, some play on words, or an absurdly simple punchline.

For example, "Why don't scientists trust atoms? Because they make up everything!" Dad jokes can also include references to pop culture or current events.

An example of this type of joke could be, "How do you make holy water? You boil the hell out of it!"

However, these types of jokes age faster than other dad jokes.

The Appeal Of Dad Jokes

One reason dad jokes have remained popular for centuries is that they are accessible to everyone. They don't require any specialized knowledge or understanding of current events to understand them.

Furthermore, even if the joke doesn't land with its intended audience, it can still make for some lighthearted ribbing between friends and family members.

This light-heartedness can create an atmosphere that encourages people to bond over shared experiences and memories—and who doesn't like that?!

There's no denying that dad jokes will always be a part of our culture—and we wouldn't want it any other way!

Whether you're telling them yourself or hearing them from someone else, there's something special about how these corny one-liners can bring people together in laughter and good times.

The history of dad jokes can be traced back to the early 20th century, when humor was a staple of family life and fathers would often tell jokes to entertain their children.

Dad Jokes Found Their Origins in the 1950s and 1960s

Dad jokes as we know them today have their roots and gained popularity in the 1950s and 1960s. They were frequently featured in popular media, such as movies and television shows.

During this time, humor was more straightforward and often relied on puns, one-liners, and gags that played off everyday life.

Jokes during this era were often told by fathers, and they often revolved around family life, work, and current events.

This style of humor was seen as lighthearted and playful, and it was a way for dads to bond with their kids and show their affection.

One common type of dad joke from this era was the groaner.

This type of joke was meant to be cheesy and over-the-top, but it was still expected to be told with a straight face. Another popular type of dad joke during this time was the one-liner.

These jokes were quick, snappy, and often relied on puns or wordplay. They were often used in casual conversation or to make light of a situation.

Jokes from this era also often poked fun at everyday life.

For example, a dad might tell a joke about his job, his family, or his hobbies. These jokes were meant to be relatable and to make people smile, even if they were a little corny.

The 1950s and 1960s laid the foundation for the dad joke as we know it today. The humor of this era was lighthearted and playful, and it was a way for dads to bond with their kids and show their affection.

The groaners, one-liners, and everyday-life jokes of this era helped establish the classic style of dad jokes that is still popular today.

Dad Jokes In Their Formative Years: 1970s and 1980s

During the 1970s and 1980s, the dad joke became a staple of popular culture, with many comedians using them as part of their routine.

The 1970s and 1980s marked a significant shift in the popularity of dad jokes.

During this time, dad jokes became a staple of popular culture and were used by many comedians as part of their routines.

With the rise of stand-up comedy and television shows, dad jokes were introduced to a wider audience and soon became a popular form of humor.

During this era, dad jokes often centered around daily life and family-oriented topics, such as parenting, marriage, and home life.

The humor was often light-hearted and wholesome, relying on puns, wordplay, and clever observations to get a laugh.

Many of the jokes from this period were based on traditional stereotypes and were designed to appeal to a broad audience.

Comedians like Bob Hope, George Burns, and Jackie Mason were known for their use of dad jokes and helped popularize the style of humor.

Additionally, television shows like The Carol Burnett Show and The Tonight Show Starring Johnny Carson helped to spread the popularity of dad jokes even further.

Overall, the 1970s and 1980s played a crucial role in shaping the modern-day dad joke and established it as a beloved form of humor that continues to be enjoyed by audiences of all ages.

Finally, the Bad Dad Jokes Evolved: Acceptance By Pop Culture of the 1990s & 2000s

In the 1990s and 2000s, the rise of the internet and social media led to an increased popularity of dad jokes, as people began to share their favorite jokes online.

During the 1990s and 2000s, the rise of the internet and social media led to an explosion in the popularity of dad jokes.

This was due to the ease with which people could now share their favorite jokes with others, regardless of location. With the click of a button, dad jokes could now be spread far and wide, reaching a new generation of joke lovers.

As a result of this increased exposure, dad jokes became a staple of popular culture, with many comedians incorporating them into their routines.

They were seen as a fun and lighthearted way to connect

with others, and the public's love for them only grew.

In addition, the rise of online humor communities, such as forums and social media groups, further fueled the popularity of dad jokes.

These communities provided a platform for people to share their own jokes, as well as to discover new ones, leading to a never-ending stream of dad jokes.

Today, dad jokes continue to be a beloved part of popular culture, with people of all ages enjoying their silly and sometimes corny humor.

Whether shared online, in person, or through comedy routines, dad jokes are here to stay, and will likely remain a staple of humor for generations to come.

In conclusion, the history of dad jokes is a long and rich one, rooted in the traditions of family life and the enduring popularity of humor.

Despite the changing times, dad jokes remain a beloved part of popular culture and continue to bring smiles to people's faces.

So recent that historians haven't had a chance to properly document it yet.

It's only been in the past few decades that the term "dad joke" has been widely used, and the trend of sharing them online has only exploded in the last few years. It's a testament to how fast humor can evolve in the age of technology.

So next time you hear a dad joke, don't groan too loudly…you might find yourself laughing along with everyone else!

JACK INK

CHAPTER 3

TYPES OF DAD JOKES

These jokes often rely on wordplay, puns, or double meanings for their humor.

No matter which type of dad joke you prefer, it's clear that these corny one-liners bring a lot of laughter and joy to family dinner tables around the world!

So don't be afraid to open your favorite dad joke book and let the good times roll! 🥏 Happy Father's Day! 🎉

Puns: Puns are a staple of dad jokes and are widely known for their clever wordplay and wit. The humor in a pun is derived from two words or phrases that sound similar but have different meanings.

This type of joke plays on the different definitions of words and phrases to create a surprising and humorous result.

For example, the joke, "What did the fish say when he hit the wall? Dam!" is a pun. The word "dam" can mean both a barrier used to control the flow of water and an exclamation of frustration.

In this joke, the pun is created by connecting the two meanings of the word "dam" humorously and unexpectedly.

Puns are a unique form of humor that require the listener to think critically and make connections between words and their multiple meanings.

This type of joke is beloved by many because it requires the listener to be an active participant in the humor and allows for a wide range of subject matter.

In the world of dad jokes, puns are a popular form of humor that is often used to make light of everyday situations and bring a smile to the faces of those around us.

Whether simple or complex, puns offer a unique and entertaining form of laughter that people of all ages can enjoy.

Double Meanings: Double meanings are a staple of dad jokes and offer a unique form of humor that appeals to people of all ages.

In these types of jokes, the words used can be understood in two different ways - literally and figuratively. This type of joke often involves a pun or play on words that create a humorous twist or surprise.

One example of a double-meaning joke is, "Why was the

math book sad? Because it had too many problems!" In this joke, "problems" can be understood as challenges or difficulties and figuratively as mathematical equations.

This creates a surprising and humorous connection between the two different meanings.

Double-meaning jokes often rely on wordplay, puns, and clever word associations to create a funny and unexpected result.

This type of humor is loved by many because it requires the listener to think critically and connect the dots between the two different meanings of the words used in the joke.

Double meanings also offer a wide range of subject matter, as they can be used to tell jokes about almost anything.

From animals to relationships, math to science, and food to sports, there is no limit to the topics that double-meaning jokes can cover.

In conclusion, double meanings are a popular and beloved form of humor that provides a unique and entertaining form of laughter.

Whether you're looking to tickle your funny bone or want to enjoy some lighthearted humor, double-meaning jokes are sure to deliver.

Witty Quips: Witty quips are also popular with dad jokes - these are clever remarks that often result in a chuckle from the audience. For example, "Did you hear about the crook who stole a calendar? He got twelve months!"

Witty quips are clever, humorous remarks that make people laugh. They are often short and to the point, and their humor is derived from their clever use of wordplay, puns, or unexpected twists.

In the context of dad jokes, witty quips play a significant role. Dad jokes are known for their cheesy, often groan-inducing humor and witty quips are the perfect tool for delivering this type of humor.

They are the backbone of the classic dad joke and are often used to set up the joke's punchline.

For example, a classic dad joke might start with a witty quip like, "Why did the tomato turn red?"

The joke setup is complete, and the listener is left wondering what the punchline will be. The answer, of course, is "Because it saw the salad dressing!"

This type of wordplay is a classic example of the type of witty quips that are used in dad jokes.

Witty quips are also used in other types of humor, such as sarcasm and irony, but they are especially prominent in dad jokes.

Their clever use of language and their ability to deliver a punchline make them the perfect tool for creating this type of humor.

So, if you're looking to add humor to your day or make someone laugh, why not try your hand at some witty quips and dad jokes?

They may not be the most sophisticated type of humor, but they are guaranteed to bring a smile and make you laugh out loud.

Corny Joke: These jokes are old and overused, making them unoriginal and predictable.

Corny jokes are a staple of the classic dad joke genre. These jokes are often cheesy, predictable, and rely on puns, word play, or a setup-punchline structure.

They are typically lighthearted and meant to be good-natured, but they can also be seen as clichéd and unoriginal.

Examples of corny jokes include:

Why did the tomato turn red?
Because it saw the salad dressing!

Why was the math book sad?
Because it had too many problems.

Why don't scientists trust atoms?
Because they make up everything.

Corny jokes are often seen as a type of humor that can appeal to a wide range of people, particularly children and families.

They can be a fun way to bring a smile to someone's face and can also be used to lighten the mood in tense situations.

However, they are not everyone's cup of tea, and some people may find them to be more eye-roll-inducing than funny.

Knock-Knock Jokes: Knock-knock jokes are a classic type of joke that has been around for generations.

They are short, simple, and easy to understand, making them a great choice for kids and adults.

The basic structure of a knock-knock joke is simple: someone says "Knock knock," and the person who hears the joke responds with "Who's there?"

The joke teller then delivers a setup, usually in the form of a pun or a play on words, and the listener responds with "Who's there?" once again. The joke's punchline is then delivered, and the listener is left to laugh or groan.

The beauty of knock-knock jokes is that they are versatile and can be adapted to fit various themes and topics.

They can be silly, absurd, or even crude, making them a great choice for various audiences. They can also be used to deliver jokes that are lighthearted and fun, as well as more serious jokes and thought-provoking.

One key thing that makes knock-knock jokes so appealing is their interactive nature. The joke teller and the listener work together to build the joke, with each person playing a crucial role in delivering the punchline.

This interactive nature makes knock-knock jokes a great choice for group settings, as everyone can take part in telling and hearing the joke.

Another great thing about knock-knock jokes is that they are easy to remember and repeat. They are short and simple, making them easy to commit to memory, and they are also easy to share with others.

Whether you're telling a joke to a friend, family member, or colleague, you can be sure that the person you're sharing it with will be able to remember the joke and share it with others in the future.

So, knock-knock jokes are a great choice whether you're a fan of silly humor, absurd jokes, or anything in between.

They are versatile, interactive, and easy to remember, making them a great choice for anyone who loves to laugh and have fun.

Popular examples of knock knock jokes include: "Knock Knock! Who's there? Boo. Boo who? Don't cry, it's just a joke!" and "Knock Knock! Who's there? Faith. Faith who? Faith you'll laugh at this joke!"

Using Dad Jokes Effectively In Conversation & Crafting Your Dad Jokes

Dad jokes have a special place in the hearts of many. They can be a great way to lighten the mood and make someone laugh, but they can also get old fast if used too often or inappropriately.

To use dad jokes effectively, you need to consider the context, avoid going overboard, and the time your joke perfectly. Let's take a look at how to do that.

Know Your Audience and Context

Knowing your audience is key when it comes to using dad jokes effectively. If you're dealing with strangers or acquaintances, it's best to avoid using overly-risqué or off-color material.

But if you're talking with friends familiar with your sense of humor and know when you're joking, feel free to let loose!

Just keep in mind that even if everyone knows each other well, there may still be certain topics that are off-limits; use caution with those types of conversations to avoid offending anyone.

Timing Is Everything

Another important factor in determining whether a joke is effective is timing – when should you tell the joke?

Look for key moments where inserting a joke might help break the tension or awkwardness in the room; this could be right after someone has said something serious or during an uncomfortable silence.

Don't try too hard; if there isn't an obvious opportunity for fun, don't force it!

Keep It Simple

Finally, simplicity is key in dad jokes; keep them short and sweet. Don't try too hard by adding unnecessary detail or making up convoluted puns – no one wants to hear an overlong punchline that takes forever to get out!

Find a good balance between using dad jokes sparingly and wearing them out; this will help ensure your jokes land without becoming annoying or repetitive.

Dad jokes are a great way to inject fun into conversations without offending anyone (if used correctly!).

Consider the context before telling any jokes and make sure you find the perfect moment for them – look for key moments of tension or awkwardness where inserting a joke can help break the ice.

Keep your dad jokes simple and avoid trying too hard by adding unnecessary detail or making up convoluted puns – no one wants an overlong punchline that takes forever to get out! With these tips in mind, you'll have everyone laughing in no time!

To Craft Your Own Dad Jokes, Follow These Steps:

1. Start with a play on words or pun. Dad jokes often use puns or play on words to create humor.

2. Keep it simple. Dad jokes are typically light and silly, so keep your joke simple and straightforward.

3. Use everyday items or situations. Dad jokes often use everyday objects, such as food or household items, as the basis for their humor.

4. Add a twist. Take a familiar situation and add a twist to it, like turning a common phrase on its head.

5. Make it silly. Dad jokes often rely on silly humor, so don't be afraid to be silly and over-the-top with your joke.

6. Use bad jokes with humor. Dad jokes often use groan-worthy jokes, so feel free to include jokes that are so bad they're good.

7. Make it relatable. Dad jokes often rely on universal experiences or situations, so try to make your joke relatable to a wide audience.

8. Practice, practice, practice! The more you practice crafting dad jokes, the better you'll become at it.

THE BAD DAD JOKE BOOK

CHAPTER 4

UNLOCKING THE MYSTERY: THE NEUROSCIENCE OF DAD JOKES AND LAUGHTER

Dad jokes have been a staple of humor for generations and have a certain type of charm that appeals to people of all ages.

But have you ever wondered what it is about these jokes that make us smile or groan in spite of ourselves?

The science behind dad jokes can be explained by the way they activate different parts of our brain.

When we hear a dad joke, our brains process the humor and pun in the joke, triggering the release of endorphins, which are the body's natural feel-good chemicals.

Additionally, the jokes often involve wordplay, which activates the language and pattern recognition centers of the brain, making us feel a sense of satisfaction when we understand the joke.

Lastly, the humor in dad jokes often involves irony and unexpected twists, which stimulates the surprise and novelty centers of the brain.

So, in essence, dad jokes are funny because they activate multiple parts of our brain, resulting in a pleasurable and satisfying experience.

The humor in dad jokes often comes from their simplicity and predictable punchline. This type of humor activates the brain's pleasure center, releasing endorphins and causing laughter.

Furthermore, dad jokes often play on word play and puns, which stimulate the language centers in the brain.

This type of humor also requires the listener to make a mental connection between two seemingly unrelated concepts, which can lead to a satisfying feeling of recognition and understanding.

The use of silly or absurd humor in dad jokes can activate the brain's sense of playfulness, making people more open to laughter and lightheartedness.

Overall, the science behind dad jokes shows that humor is a complex and multi-layered process that can bring joy and laughter to people of all ages.

Another aspect of the science behind dad jokes and laughter is the psychological and emotional benefits it provides.

Laughter has been shown to reduce stress, boost mood, and improve overall well-being.

The brain releases endorphins, the body's natural painkillers, during laughter which leads to feelings of happiness and relaxation.

Additionally, laughter has been shown to improve cognitive functions such as memory, creativity, and problem-solving skills.

In the case of dad jokes, their predictable, yet humorous nature, triggers the release of endorphins, providing the teller and listener with the benefits of laughter.

Sharing a dad joke with someone can also help strengthen social bonds and foster a sense of community.

CHAPTER 5

THE DAD JOKE DILEMMA

Is The Humor In These Jokes Just In The Eye Of The Beholder?

We've all been there. You're at a family gathering or out with friends, and someone cracks a dad joke. And even though you know, it's probably going to be terrible; you still laugh because they're your dad.

But are dad jokes that funny? Or are we just laughing because we have to? Let's explore the humor in these so-called dad jokes and see if we can figure out once and for all if they're funny.

A Dad Joke Is A Timeless Form Of Humor Passed Down From Generation To Generation

Dad jokes have been around for as long as we can remember, wreaking havoc on the ones we love with their terrible-yet-hilarious punchlines. Their simplistic nature is their greatest asset.

All that's required to understand a dad joke is a basic sense of humor, ensuring everyone in the room can enjoy them. When mom isn't around, and it's just dad, you know it will be a wild ride filled with puns and groans.

Whether you like them or not, you have to admit dad jokes never go out of style - they are truly a timeless form of humor!

But What About These Jokes That Make Them So Funny, And Why Do They Seem To Be The Butt Of So Many Jokes Themselves?

It's often said that money might not buy you love, but it can certainly buy a lot of laughter.

While comedians continue to mine gold from their jokes about lawyers and the legal profession, one of the reasons they've struck such a rich vein with these gags is due to the seriousness and dullness of much of the work these professionals undertake.

This juxtaposition between mundane and comedy helps make lawyer jokes so funny - even if the self-same people don't particularly find them amusing.

Whether it's an examination of gender or a reflection on human nature, humor can always be found in any occupation – lawyers included!

Are Dad Jokes Just A Matter Of Taste, Or Is There Something More To Them That We Can All Appreciate?

Dad jokes are like marmite; you either love them or hate them.

But for those who enjoy a good dad joke, there is something else to be appreciated, the effort behind every bad pun, embarrassing pun, and even completely obvious punchline!

While dads take great pride in their jokes, it's not just about having an eye for comedy - there's always an element of showing off involved when pulling off the perfect dad joke!

With practice and dedication, anyone can master the art of making others groan with laughter...or roll their eyes.

It all depends on how the Dad Joke is received! So here's to Dad jokes everywhere; keep pushing those boundaries!

A Closer Look At The Dad Joke And See If We Can Figure Out What Makes Them So Special - And Maybe Even Laugh At A Few Along The Way!

Dad jokes have long been the sufferers of a bad rap. The joke that brings laughter to children and embarrassment to parents is often met with an eye roll or two.

But, if you take the time to dive deeper, there's something rather special about them.

While some dad jokes may be on the lame side, they make us laugh for another reason – because of the joy coming from spending time and connecting with our fathers.

No matter how oft-used and familiar the joke may be, it's a reminder of home (perhaps even a fond memory!) when our dads pulled out their favorite one-liners.

For that reason, we don't stop ourselves from giggling, which reinforces why dad jokes are so loved!

JACK INK

CHAPTER 6

IT'S A LAUGH-FEST

Who Can Benefit from Pun-tastic Fun

Get ready to let out a few chuckles (or guffaws).

Sometimes all you need to end a hard day is a good laugh. But did you know that there are real benefits to laughing and cracking puns? So what are these benefits, and who can benefit from the lightheartedness of puns?

Read on for the answers. Laughing has been shown to boost our mood and immune system, reduce stress levels, help us better handle pain, and even cause positive physical changes in our brains, creating more neural pathways.

Puns also offer loads of mental benefits such as improved language skills, enhanced creativity and problem-solving abilities, improved communication skills, increased resilience to life's inevitable setbacks, and helping to build better relationships.

Everyone stands to gain from laughter and punny fun, no matter what age or background they come from. Kids can use it as a tool for learning new words in creative ways.

For teens, it can provide moments of relaxation during times of stress.

Adults use it as an opportunity for connection with their friends and co-workers, while seniors find that it helps them reinvigorate old memories or engage with younger generations.

So, when the pressures of life get too intense for you or your family members or loved ones – don't forget about the power of laughter and punning! They could be just what you need for some much-needed relief.

CHAPTER 7

CLASSIC DAD JOKES FOR EVERYONE

Dad jokes have been around for centuries, passed down through generations, and used to bring laughter into conversations.

This chapter looks at some classic dad jokes that everyone can appreciate.

No matter the occasion, dad jokes can add some lighthearted humor to any conversation. And now that you've read some of the classic dad jokes, why not try them?

Remember to use them sparingly and at the right moments; soon enough, you'll have everyone in stitches!

Dad jokes have been a timeless form of humor, appreciated by people of all ages. Embrace your inner dad and spread joy and laughter.

How do you fix a broken tomato? With tomato paste!

Why did the scarecrow win an award? Because he was outstanding in his field!

Why did the cow jump over the moon? Because the farmer had cold hands!

What kind of cheese do you use to disguise a horse? Mask-a-pony!

How do you make an octopus laugh? With ten-tickles!

Why did the computer keep sneezing? It had a virus!

Why did the banana go to the hospital? Because it was feeling a-peel-ing!

Why did the mouse eat a clock? He wanted to have more time!

What do you call a bear with no teeth? A toothless grizzly - or a cuddly gummy!

Where do animals go when their tail falls off? To the retail store!

How are false teeth like stars? They both come out at night!

What do you call a dog with no front legs?
Wobbles!

What did one elevator say to the other
elevator? I think I'm going down!

What did one firefly say to the other firefly?
Lighten up!

Why did the tomato blush? Because he saw
the salad dressing!

How do you make an elephant float? You use
two scoops of ice cream and a large straw!

How do trees get online? They log in!

What did one eye say to the other eye?
Between us, something smells!

Why did the cookie go to the doctor?
Because it was feeling crummy!

What do you call a snake that only says no? A
Negative Nelly!

Why did the bee go to the dentist? Because it
needed a hum filling!

How do you get an octopus to smile? Give
him eight reasons why!

What did the fish say when it ran out of

water? "This just doesn't make scents!"

Why didn't the bicycle stand up on its own? It was two tired!

Why did the couch fall asleep during math class? It was too bored by all the equations!

What did the farmer say when he saw a jalapeno pepper? "Hot stuff comin' through!"

How do you make a tissue dance? You put a little boogie in it!

What did the electrical outlet say to the plug? "You light up my life!"

What did one wall say to the other wall? "I've got my eye on you!"

Where do birds go for a drink after work? To the feather factory! 1

Why don't skeletons ever go out on dates? Because they don't have any guts!

How did the scarecrow win the Nobel Prize? He was outstanding in his field!

Why don't elephants take up skating? Because they can't get the hang of it!

What did the janitor say when he jumped out

of the closet? "Hey everyone, surprise!"

What did the rock say when it rolled down the hill? "I'm on a roll!"

Where do chickens go to deposit their money? The egg-bank!

What does a bee do when it's sad? It takes a buzzer pill!

How does an astronaut stay warm in outer space? By orbiting closer to the sun!

Why did Tarzan quit his job as an investment banker? He didn't know how to jungle money matters!

What did one eye say to the other eye? Between us, something smells!

Why was the giraffe kicked out of the bank? He had a lot of high-interest loans!

What did one pillow say to the other pillow? "You can call me a couch potato if you want!"

Why didn't the zombie go to work? He was feeling un-dead tired!

Why don't scientists trust atoms? Because they make up everything and you never know what they're going to do next!

How do you wake up a sleeping bear? You don't. You run and hope he's still asleep when you get there!

What did the traffic light say to the car? "Don't look. I'm changing!"

What did the computer do at lunchtime? He had a byte and went back to work!

Why didn't Cheshire Cat use her cell phone? She didn't have enough purr-ception!

What did one say to the other calculator? "You can count on me!"

How does a sea lion keep his hair slicked back? With sealant!

What do you call an alligator in a vest? An Investi-gator!

How do you make a tissue dance? You put a little boogie in it!

What did the DNA strand say after being copied? "Gimme some space. I feel replicated!"

Why was the math book sad? Because it had

so many problems!

What do you call an alligator in a suit? A courtroom croc!

What did one onion say to the other onion? We'll have to make crystals and crystalize together!

What did the clock do when it was time for the dentist appointment? It struck toothache!

What did the banana say to the apple? "You look sooooo good. I could peel off!"

Why did the chicken go to the party? To get clucked up!

How does an astronaut know when he is hungry? When his stomach starts to orbit!

What did the one oven say to the other oven? "You are too hot to handle!"

What did the turtle say when he saw his reflection in the mirror? "Wow, I look shell-licious!"

How do you make a dragon laugh? Tell it a joke it's never heard before!

Why did one shoe go to the party alone? His

date was a flip-flop!

Why don't cows like fast food? Because they can't catch it!

Why did the scarecrow go to the movie alone? He wanted to see a field of dreams!

Why did the golfer wear two pairs of pants? So he could have a spare if the first one got a hole in it!

What did one calculator say to the other calculator? "You can count on me!"

Why did one shoe go to the party alone? His date was a flip-flop!

What did one oven say to the other oven? "You are too hot to handle!"

What did one onion say to the other onion? "We'll have to make like crystals and crystalize together!"

What did one plate say to the other plate? "Let's make a night out of it - break out the good silverware!"

Where do lawyers learn how to sue people? Law school!

JACK INK

CHAPTER 8

THE BEST PUNS, KNOCK-KNOCKS AND ONE LINERS

Whether you're a pun enthusiast or just looking for some laughs, this chapter is filled with endless amounts of wit and hilarity.

Here you'll find the best puns, funniest knock-knocks, and wittiest one-liners that will have you in stitches.

Jokes are a universal language, they bring people together and lighten the mood. With a good joke, you can instantly turn a bad day into a good one.

Dad jokes are no exception, they are the epitome of cheesy humor and are guaranteed to bring a smile to your face.

These jokes may be simple, but they are timeless and have been passed down through generations.

Whether you're telling them to your friends, family, or complete strangers, dad jokes never fail to bring a laugh

Get ready to laugh until you ache, because this chapter is packed with puns that will tickle your funny bone!

My daughter asked if she could play the violin, and I said yes, so now we have many strings attached!

How do lawyers say goodbye in court? They objectively remark!

What did the carrot say to the broccoli? I feel like we're stalks apart!

What did the grape say when it got stepped on? Nothing—it just let out a little wine!

My dad said he would be a comedian, but then he changed his mind… He decided to be an accountant instead…

How do lawyers say goodbye in court? They objectively remark!

Why can't you trust stairs? They always tell tales!

Why did the frog go to the bank? He wanted to get some croaks!

Where do sheep go on holiday? The Baaaaaahamas!

What did the left eye say to the right eye? Between you and me, something smells!

What did one elevator say to the other? I'm coming down with something!

What did one toilet say to the other? You look a bit flushed!

Why did the mushroom ask for a raise from his boss? He wanted to be an 'above average' fungi!

What kind of jokes do bees tell each other? Buzz-words!

What's a pirate's favorite letter? Arrrghhhh!!

What did one thermometer say to the other? You make my temperature rise!

How do you make a tissue dance? You put a little boogie in it!

Why don't seagulls fly inland? They don't want to hang around with landgulls!

Where do pencils go on vacation? Pencil-Vania!

What did the refrigerator say when someone opened its door? Close the door. I'm feeling cold!

Did you hear the joke about the roof? Never

mind - it's over your head!

How does a train eat? It goes chew, chew!

How do ships communicate with each other? They use morse code!

What did one traffic light say to the other? Don't look. I'm changing colors!

Why are ghosts so bad at lying? Because you can see right through them!

Knock, knock! Who's there? Boo. Boo who? Don't cry. It's only a joke!

What did the egg say to the boiling water? It might take me a while, but I'll get hard soon!

Why do trees make poor students? They don't branch out!

Why did the two blondes keep running in circles? They were trying to find their way back!

What did the hammer say to the nail? Give me a pound, and we'll call it even!

What do you call someone who steals an alphabet? A thieftist!

How do you fix a broken pizza? With tomato

paste!

What did one elevator say to the other elevator? I'm going down with this relationship!

Why can't you trust stairs? Because they're always up to something!

What did the candle say to its mom? Don't worry. I'm feeling wicked!

How do you talk to a skyscraper? With lots of elevation!

Why did the dad throw the baby and the rubber duck out with the bath water? He wanted to make sure the bath toys got a good rinse too!

Did you hear about the bed that was arrested? It didn't put up any resistance!

Why did the student eat his homework? He wanted to get an A-plus-stomach-ache!

Did you hear about the man who invented helicopters? He was a real whirlybird!

Why don't astronauts ever get hungry on long flights? Because they brought their launch codes!

What did the onion say when it was sliced? Nothing, it just kept crying!

What did the scarecrow win at the talent show? A first-caw prize!

Why don't cannibals eat clowns? Because they taste funny!

How do you organize a space party? You planet!

What did the frog order at the restaurant? French flies and a diet croak!

Why did the tomato blush? Because she saw the salad dressing coming!

What did the traffic light say to the car? Don't look. I'm changing!

What did one volcano say to the other? Are you erupting too?!

How do crazy scientists organize their labs? By periodic laughter!

What did the yogi say when he went to lunch? Om nom nom nom!

Why was the math book so sad? Because it had so many problems!

Where do snowmen dance? To a snowball disco!

Why don't robots tell jokes? They don't get the punchlines!

With my daughter's math problem, I reach a dead end every time.

Having a conversation with my teenage daughter is like playing chess with a pigeon - no matter how many moves ahead I plan, it just knocks over the pieces and struts about victorious.

You know your relationship has gotten serious when your alarm goes off in the morning, and you both look away, pretending you didn't hear it.

So my son asked me why the moon looks different all the time. I told him that even in space, fashion trends come and go!

If money did grow on trees, that would be something to bark about!

Knock, knock! Who's there? Orange. Orange who? Orange you surprised to hear a knock-knock joke?

Knock, knock! Who's there? Ketchup.

Ketchup who? Catch up with me later, and we'll have a chat!

Knock, knock! Who's there? Police. Police who? Police let me in already - it's freezing out here!

Knock, knock! Who's there? Noah. Noah who? Noah good place to find jokes around here?!

Knock, knock! Who's there? Ice cream. Ice cream who? I scream for more jokes like these!!

Knock, knock! Who's there? Howard. Howard who? Howard you know if you don't laugh at this joke?!

Knock, knock! Who's there? Anya. Anya who? Anya chance of a smile after this joke?!

Knock, knock! Who's there? Tank. Tank who? You're welcome - now come on in!

Knock, knock! Who's there? Jeans. Jeans who? Genes not jeans - time for some new material!!

Knock, knock! Who's there? Karma. Karma who? Karma got what I deserve already – a bad joke!!

Knock, knock. Who's there? Wanda. Wanda who? Wanda you going to open the door or what?

Knock, knock. Who's there? Hatch. Hatch who? Bless you! No wait, that's the wrong joke... hatch you ready for a good time?

Knock, knock. Who's there? Nobel. Nobel who? No bell, that's why I'm knocking!

Why did the frog call his insurance company? He had a jump in his car.

What do you call an elf who has run away from the North Pole? A rebellious dwarf.

What do you call a snowman with a six-pack? An abdominal snowman.

Why did the chicken cross the playground? To get to the other slide.

What do you call a horse that can play an instrument? A hoof-tastic musician.

What do you call a giraffe wearing a turtleneck? A stretch neck.

Why don't oysters share their pearls?

Because they're shellfish!

What do you call a penguin in the desert?
Lost.

Why did the elephant paint its toenails red?
So it could hide in the cherry tree!

What do you call a magician who has run away from the circus? A disappearing act.

Why did the bicycle fall over? It was two tired!

What do you call a frog who has flown the coop? An amphibian escapee.

Why did the duck cross the road? To prove he wasn't a chicken.

What do you call a fish that's out of water and has no home? A lost soul!

Why did the scarecrow win an award? He was outstanding in his field.

What do you call an alligator wearing a bowtie? A dressed-up reptile.

Why did the cookie go to the doctor?
Because it felt crumbly.

What do you call a bear who can sing? A

harmonious grizzly.

What's a fish's favorite movie? Anything with a little bite!

What do you call a group of cows playing instruments? A moo-sical band.

Why do trees always tell the truth? Because they have roots.

CHAPTER 9

CLEAN, WHOLESOME FUN FOR FAMILIES EVERYWHERE

If you're looking for a way to bring laughter and smiles to your home, then look no further.

Here you'll find only the best clean jokes and gags that will get everyone in your family— from the youngest to the oldest—laughing out loud!

So take a break from technology and enjoy some good old-fashioned entertainment with the ones you love.

What did the parent tree say to the baby tree? "Grow up!"

What do you call a fake noodle? An Impasta!

How do you communicate with a fish? You drop it a line.

What did the cow say when it fell into the ditch? "Mooooooove!"

Why don't eggs tell jokes? They'd crack each other up!

What did the fish say when it saw the submarine? "Nothing, it just waved!

Why don't crabs give to charity? Because they're shellfish.

Why does Snoop Dogg carry an umbrella everywhere he goes? Fo' drizzle

Why did the bee get rejected from the school spelling bee? Because he was just a little too buzzy!

How do you make an octopus laugh? You tickle its tentacles!

What did one ghost say to the other when they passed in the hallways? "Boo!"

Why don't mathematicians mind their own business? Because they know it's all relative!

Why can't you trust politicians in the wintertime? They tend to flip-flop on their decisions!

What do you call a fly without wings? A walk!

How does a scientist freshen their breath? With experi-mints!

Why don't scientists trust stairs? Because they always get tripped up on them!

Why did the scarecrow win an award? Because he was outstanding in his field!

What kind of key opens a banana? A monkey!

Why did the couch leave the party early? He was feeling all "tufted" out!

Where do cows go for entertainment? The moo-vies!

Why doesn't history repeat itself? Because we don't listen!

Why don't scientists play hide and seek anymore? Nobody can find them!

What did the mirror say to the wall? Is there

anyone else around here who's better looking than me?!

What did one eye say to the other? Between you and me, something's not quite right!

Why don't scientists take coffee breaks? They don't want to decrease their productivity!

How do mathematicians eat their dinner? With a protractor and ruler!

What do you call a cow after it's delivered a new calf? Decalfinated!

What do lawyers wear to court? Lawsuits!

Why don't crows tell jokes? Because they aren't corvous enough!

What did the dinosaur do when his phone bill was too high? He turned off his roars!

What did one contact lens say to the other? Lenses together forever!

How do cats greet each other? Meowy Christmas!

Why don't scientists like being close to each other? They repel each other's ideas!

What did one magnet say to the other? I find

you very attractive!

How do astronomers organize their parties?
They planet!

Why don't scientists tell lies? Because they
can't keep things labeled properly!

What did one mountain say to the other
mountain? I'm hill-arious!

Why don't mathematicians like distractions?
Because they can't solve any problems with
them around!

Why did the mummy go on vacation? To
wrap up some rest and relaxation!

What did the tree say when it was cut down?
Timber!!!

Why don't scientists take vacations? They
don't know how to relax without an
experiment!

Why does a computer always sound excited
about work? Because it's always getting a
byte out of it!

What did one wall say to the other wall when
it was knocked down? Don't worry. I'll be
back up soon enough!

What kind of cake do scientists make best? A test tube cake!

How does an alien man ask for his lady's hand in marriage? Take me to your leader!

What did the little monster do when his parents didn't believe him? He raised hell!

Why don't scientists trust each other? Because they can't keep their secrets under wraps!

What's worse than finding a worm in your apple? Finding half of one!

How do cats tell time? By meowing twice an hour!

What did one wall say to the other wall when it was knocked down? Don't worry. I'll be back up soon enough!

What did one oven mitt say to the other oven mitt? Let's get hot tonight!

Why is six afraid of 7? Because 7 8 9.

What did one computer chip say to the other computer chip? Nothing, they never store anything together!

What did one eye patch say to the other eye patch? We both see eye to eye!

Why did the attorney cross the street? To give the bar a little legal representation!

What sets apart a legal pro from a legal genius? A legal pro knows the law, but a legal genius knows the judge's coffee order.

Why do sharks never mess with lawyers? They have a strict code of lawyer-shark ethics.

What do lawyers call their favorite animal? A "legal-eagle"

Why did the attorney bring a lazy boy to court? To give his arguments a restful touch!

What's the definition of a bummer? A room full of lawyers with no power source.

Why did the attorney carry a green pen? To sign off on a plea bargain and show his eco-consciousness!

What's the difference between a dead skunk on the road and a dead lawyer on the road? The skid marks in front of the skunk show it tried to avoid the collision.

Why did the lawyer bring a ladder to court?
To reach a higher judgment!

JACK INK

CHAPTER 10

HILARIOUS RESPONSES TO EVERYDAY SITUATIONS

Here you'll find the best zingers and comebacks that will leave your friends and family in stitches. Ever been caught off guard by a tricky question or an unexpected challenge?

Well, look no further—this chapter is full of one-liners and witty remarks that will have you prepared for any situation. So sharpen your wit and get ready for some fun!

The hipster was feeling the heat when he sipped his coffee – he had taken it before it became trendy!

Want to hear a piano joke? Sure, hit me with it!

What do you call a sleeping bull? A bulldozer!

Why don't oysters give to charity? Because their shells are too tight and frugal!

Why can't astronauts eat during launch? They're under too much pressure!

What do you call a dad who likes to cook? A sauté daddy!

Why did the dad decide to stay home from work? He had a "low battery" and needed to recharge!

What did the dad say when he found out his daughter was going to college? "She'll be able to bring home the bacon now!"

Where do dads go on vacation when they want some rest? The father-in-law suite!

What do dads like on their pizza? Father-in-laws!

What kind of music does a cool dad like to listen to? Daddy rap!

When does a dad know it's time for bed at night? When he has motion sensors activated in all his rooms!

What did the father tell his daughter before he tucked her in bed each night? Sleep tight, and don't let the bed bugs bite your wallet!

Why are computers so popular with dads? Because they have all the user-friendly shortcuts!

When two fathers argue over which parenting style works best, what do you call? A Dad debate!

Why do most fathers enjoy shopping online with their children so much? Because they can get free delivery fees anytime!

Why did the dad cross the road? Get to the second-hand store and save money!

How do you confuse a new dad? Ask him where the diaper changing station is!

What do dads bring to a party that no one else does? A sense of responsibility and order!

Where do dads like to hang out after work? The mancave!

What did the dad say when his daughter told him she was going to law school? "I knew you'd be good at arguing your case!"

What did the dad say when his son said he wanted to be an astronaut when he grew up? "You can reach for the sky. Just make sure you come back down before dinner!"

What did the nacho cheese say to the tortilla chips? Nothing, they just cheesy smiled at each other.

Did you hear the one about the scientist who had to explain quantum physics to his dad? He said, "It's simple, dad—don't think too hard, or you'll end up in a parallel universe!"

What do you call a dad who loves music? A tune-in father.

Why did the ketchup bottle refuse to give his notes back? He didn't want someone else stealing his sauces.

What did one egg say to the other egg after he made a bad joke? "Whatever, yolk!"

What did one leaf say to another leaf as they

were falling from a tree? "Let's keep our fingers crossed for a soft landing!"

Why don't pirates ever get sick? Because they always remember to take their parrot-a-ceuticals!

Why don't trees tell jokes while they are skiing? Because they can't stop laughing long enough to finish them!

What do you call a bee that's patriotic to the USA? An USB, or a United States Bee!

How much does a hipster weigh? An Instagram!

What did one banana say to the other banana? "Let's split this shake!"

What do you call a dad who's good at telling dirty jokes? A pun-father!

What did the dad say when he found out his daughter had pierced her nose? Nose how to pick 'em!

How many dads does it take to screw in a lightbulb? One—he holds it up, and the world revolves around him!

Why do mommies love dad jokes so much?

They remind them of their own husbands!

What did the kid say when his dad asked him to rake the leaves in the backyard? I'm leaf it all up to you!

Why are dads always making jokes instead of doing work? Because they'd rather be funny than useful!

Why did Dad set two alarm clocks in the morning? He wanted to make sure he was twice as woke!

What's Dad's favorite kind of music? Heavy metal - because nothing rocks like Dad's jokes!

Why did the dad cross the road? Because his kids told him not to.

What did the dad say when his son asked for a new bike? If I had two, I'd give you one!

What do you call a dad with five children? A skillful multiplier!

What did the father say to his daughter when she was acting up? "If you keep that up, I'm going to make sure you have enough siblings to form a band!"

Why is it so hard for dads to remember birthdays? They haven't done it nearly as much as mothers have!

How do dads mark special occasions? By using a permanent marker!

What do you call an older man with a bunch of kids running around him? Dad of the year

Why did the dad take a break while watching TV with his kids? He needed some commercial-free time!

Who always has the best puzzles and riddles at family gatherings? Dad, of course!

Seagulls soar above the ocean – that's where they get their name! If they flew over the bay, they'd have to be called 'bagels'!

What is a pirate's favorite letter? You'd think it would be the C-capital R, but it's actually the Arrr!

I used to work in a shoe factory, but it was a soul-crushing job.

What did one plate say to the other plate? Dinner is on me!

Two guys walk into a bar. You would think

one of them would have seen it.

I woke up from my dream thinking I had devoured a giant marshmallow, only to realize my pillow was nowhere in sight!

A man strolled into a library looking for a book on how to defy gravity - instead, he ended up being fined for overdue books!

What did the dad say to his daughter after he caught her smoking? "I'm not mad. I just can't believe you inhaled."

How do dad's like their eggs? Fertilized.

What did the daughter say when her father asked why she was on her phone all night? "Sorry I wasn't answering your calls—I was playing solitaire."

What did the dad tell his son when he asked to borrow the car? "We'll see if you can make it out of the driveway first!"

Why did the dad threaten to throw his son's Xbox out of the window? He wanted him to get some fresh air and exercise!

Why couldn't the dad watch his favorite TV show anymore? His daughter changed all the channels!

Why didn't the dad want any more children? His last one gave him grey hair!

What did the daughter say when she saw her father walking into her room at night? "It's 2 am--you know what they say: 'never trust a Dad past 10 pm.' "

Why did the dad joke change his mind about having more kids? He heard that two is twice as much trouble!

What did the dad tell his son when he asked for an allowance? "Son, money doesn't grow on trees, but I think I can spare some pocket change."

What did the dad say when his daughter asked if she could borrow his car? "We'll see if you can jumpstart it first!"

Why couldn't the dad keep up with his son in a race? He got tired of chasing after him!

What did the dad say to his son when he asked for the car keys? "Not so fast—you need to show me you can handle a scooter first!"

How do you tell if something is hot on the internet? It's "going viral!"

JACK INK

CHAPTER 11

HISTORY LESSONS WITH AN ADDED PINCH OF HUMOR

You'll find a unique twist on traditional history lessons. We've added some good old-fashioned dad jokes to the mix to make learning about historical events even more fun.

Learning about history doesn't have to be dull. With the added bonus of dad jokes, you can make history lessons even more enjoyable!

Discover some of the most interesting and noteworthy people, places, and events in history – with a good laugh every now and then.

From Ancient Greece to the 20th century, these entertaining accounts of history will take you all around the world – while bringing a smile to your face!

Did you know the internet was invented in the 20th century? Yeah, but it felt like an eternity waiting for it to load!

Why did they call it the World War I? Apparently they ran out of ideas after that one!

What did people do in the days before computers existed? Believe it or not, they had to actually talk to each other face-to-face!

How did the Cold War end? It was too chilly for anyone to stick around!

What did the ancient Egyptians say when they caught a cold? Pharaoh!

Why couldn't the Romans build a wall? Because all their rocks were called Pompeii!

What did Charlemagne say after he conquered Europe? Francly, I'm impressed!

What did the farmer say about losing his cow in the Civil War? Mooo-mento Mori!

How did Alexander the Great start his day? With a Macedonian breakfast!

What did Machiavelli say when his recipe

didn't turn out right? The end never justifies the measure!

What did Queen Elizabeth I use to clean her castle? A mop of Tudor roses!

Why was Attila the Hun so difficult to sack? Because he was always on the attack!

Why didn't Julius Caesar like taking the bus? Too many stops, and Roman waits!

Why was the Ancient Greek philosopher so good at chess? Because he was a master of logic!

What did Genghis Khan use for Twitter? Yammer!

Why did the Romans take so long to build higher walls? Too much cement-us oppidanum!

What did the sailors on Christopher Columbus' ship do when they wanted to watch TV? They invented reality TV!

How did King Henry VIII stop his hair from getting tangled? He used a royal detangler!

Why was Julius Caesar so good at financial planning? He was an expert in frugality!

What did the ancient Egyptian pharaohs use to play a game of squash? A pyramid racket!

How did Queen Victoria know when it was safe to go swimming? She consulted her tide analyst!

Why could the knights in King Arthur's court never win at chess? They only knew how to castle, mate!

What did Attila the Hun use for public transport? His own chariot of fire!

Why did Julius Caesar cross the Rubicon River? To get to the other side!

What do you call a time traveler who's always late? A history procrastinator.

Why did Cleopatra have such long fingernails? She was queen of the nail-biters.

What do you call a knight who's always on time? Sir Prompt-a-lot.

Why did George Washington chop down the cherry tree? He wanted to make a point!

What do you call an Egyptian king who's always hungry? Pharaoh-n-eat.

Why did the Pilgrims come to America? To start a fresh baste.

What do you call a Roman who's always sleepy? A doze-ian.

Why did Marie Curie discover radium? She was glowing with excitement.

What do you call a pirate who's always well-read? Captain Literature.

Why did Leonardo da Vinci invent the flying machine? He wanted to soar the skies of imagination!

What do you call a Renaissance artist who's always in a hurry? Michelangelo in a minute.

Why did Christopher Columbus set sail for the New World? He was tired of being landlocked.

What do you call a cowboy who's always well-dressed? A stylish wrangler.

Why did the Wright brothers invent the airplane? They wanted to reach for the skies!

What do you call a Viking who's always on time? Norse-a-punctual.

Why did King Tut have so many treasures? He was a true Pharaoh-n-t.

What do you call a Roman emperor who's always hungry? Nero-n-eat.

Why did Julius Caesar invade Gaul? He wanted to conquer new territory!

What do you call a Greek philosopher who's always happy? A cheerful-ist.

Why did the Roman Empire fall? Because it couldn't handle the weight!

What do you call an Egyptian pharaoh who's always cold? King Chilly-ramesses.

Why did Genghis Khan conquer so many lands? He was always on the hunt for empire-building opportunities!

What do you call a medieval knight who's always hungry? Sir-loin.

Why did the Mona Lisa smile? Because she heard a great Leonardo da Vinci joke!

What do you call a time traveler who's always sleepy? A nap-a-listic historian.

Why did Cleopatra join the Roman Empire?

She wanted to be part of the in-Pharaoh-
nment.

What do you call a pirate who's always late?
Captain Slowpoke.

Why did the first settlers come to America?
They wanted to start a new colo-nation.

What do you call a cowboy who's always sad?
A blue-jean wrangler.

What do you call a time traveler who's
always hungry? A history buff-et.

Why did King Henry VIII have so many
wives? He was looking for the perfect Henry-
mony.

What do you call a knight who's always
afraid? Sir-venturous.

Why did George Washington chop down the
cherry tree? He was in a chop-stick mood!

What do you call a pirate who's always cold?
Captain Chill-beard.

Why did the Pilgrims come to America? To
escape the cooking in-gredi-ents in England.

What do you call a Roman who's always hotheaded? An angry-an.

Why did Marie Curie discover radium? She was always shining with curiosity!

What do you call a Greek philosopher who's always late? An always-late-istic.

JACK INK

CHAPTER 12

SPORTS JOKES FOR DADS WHO LOVE TO WATCH A GAME

Dads, get ready for some laughs! This collection of sports jokes is sure to make you chuckle.

Sports jokes are a great way to lighten the mood and make your next game night more enjoyable.

Whether you're watching football, baseball, hockey or basketball, it can be fun to poke some good-natured ribbing at your favorite athletes.

This chapter brings together a collection of sports jokes that will have you laughing in no time! So get ready for some ribbing fun with your friends and family as you enjoy the game!

These funny lines will give your good-natured ribbing an extra kick, whether it's football, baseball, hockey, basketball, or any other sport.

So get ready to make some fun of your favorite athletes and enjoy a good laugh with your buddies!

Why did the punter kick the referee? He was hoping for a 15-yard penalty!

What did the basketball say when it got lost? "I'm hoopless!"

Why did the baseball fan want to return to his seat? So he could catch up on all the innings!

What do you call an over-competitive soccer player? A goal hog!

Did you hear about the goalie who changed teams every week? He wanted to be a free agent.

What do you call a basketball player who can't shoot straight? A free thrower!

Why did the chicken cross the baseball field? So he could get to home plate!

Why did the golfer wear two pairs of pants? In case he got a hole-in-one!

Why does everyone in golf wear white? So it looks like the grass has more friends.

Why did the basketball teams switch courts? They wanted to get the home-court advantage!

Why was the coach mad at the baseball team? He just found out they've been stealing bases!

What do they call a touchdown dance in baseball? A homerun jig!

How can you tell if someone is playing volleyball? Look for two net losses.

Why don't scientists play basketball? Because they always get stumped by laboratory equipment."

Where do football coaches hold their meetings? In an end zone.

Can someone please explain why golfers always wear golf hats while they play? It's to keep them from getting sun strokes!

Can someone please explain why hockey teams always flip coins before games begin? It's to make sure no teams try to take over ice time!

How can you tell if someone is playing tennis at night? Look for nighttime services.

What do you call a soccer match between two

teams of toddlers? A Pee Wee League!

What position does a hockey player take when no one is looking? A breakaway!

Where do tennis players go on vacation? The court-try!

Why do soccer fans keep scoring during each game? Because they want to stay in touch with their goals.

Why do soccer teams always practice together? They want to keep in sync with their goals.

Why don't golfers play cards? Because there are too many clubs in their bag!

Why was the basketball player refusing to leave the court? He didn't want to be called for traveling!

Why were the football players so excited about going on vacation together? Because they all wanted to touchdown in paradise!

What did one golfer say to the other golfer after he had hit a great shot? Nice drive!

What did one golfer say to the other golfer after hearing their bad lie? That's too bad - I guess it's par for the course!

What did the fencing coach say when his team won the championship? We should all be proud of our pointy performance!

Why did the athlete quit running track? He wanted to go into lane change.

Why did the basketball player run off the court when he saw two people arguing? He thought it was foul play!

Why was the baseball team so excited when they got back to the locker room? They had just hit a home run!

Why was the coach so mad at his volleyball team? He just found out they didn't know how to set!

Why won't baseball players play in the rain? They don't want to get caught in a slip-slide!

Do golfers ever take breaks during their rounds? Yep - They always take mulligans!

What did they name this year's championship trophy in Ice Hockey? The Icicle Cup!

What did they name this year's

championship trophy in Racquetball? The Racketeer!

What does a swimmer always say before diving into the pool? Ready, Set, Splash!

Where do lacrosse players go on vacation? The Stick Islands!

Why don't fishermen play golf anymore? All their rods were getting bent!

JACK INK

CHAPTER 13

MATH & SCIENCE JOKES FOR THE BRAINIAC SPOKEN IN PLAIN ENGLISH

Whether you're an adult who loves to laugh or a kid with a love for math and science, these bad dad jokes will have you rolling with laughter!

From Newtonian physics to calculus, the world of math and science can be intimidating - but it doesn't have to be!

Laughter is one of the most powerful tools in the world, so why not make use of it? Bad dad jokes related to math and science provide a fun way to lighten up any classroom or study session.

So what are you waiting for? Get out there and share some bad dad jokes today!

Math and science can be serious disciplines - but that doesn't mean you can't have a good laugh!

Whether you're an adult who loves to giggle, or a kid with a passion for numbers and equations, bad dad jokes are sure to bring the funny.

From silly puns to light-hearted one-liners, these math and science dad jokes are sure to leave you in stitches!

Are scientists good at problem-solving? You better believe it – they have plenty of Ph.D.s in that!

Did you hear what happened when two atoms collided? They shared electrons and became friends!

Did you hear what happened when two protons collided? Their mutual attraction was undeniable!

Do scientists always get along with their peers? Absolutely – there's always a strong affinity between them!

How do you know a mathematician loves coffee? Because they can always solve for a latte.

How does a physicist measure physical beauty? By counting her energy levels.

How does an astronomer show his affection? By giving supernovas and shooting stars.

What did one atom say when asked about its favorite color? I'm positively charged towards pink!

What did one DNA molecule tell another on their first date? You've got my helicase spinning!

What did one electron say to his partner at a club? Let's boogie down and ionize this place!

What did one electron say to the other during an experiment? We have to keep a positive charge!

What did one electron say to the other when they were lost? Quick, let's orbit around and find our way out!

What did one electron say when his friend was feeling down? Take a proton, and everything will be alright!

What did one light particle say to the other when they first met? It's so bright to meet you!

What did one nucleus say to the other when they were in love? We have a really strong binding force!

What did one proton say to another after a chemistry test? We passed with flying colors!

What did the particle physicist say when she made a great breakthrough? It's positively charged with excitement!

What does a physicist do when he needs to make a decision? He refers to his trusty period table!

What is an astronomer's favorite type of jewelry? Asteroid rings!

When two molecules make it official, what do they become? Covalent bonds!

Why did a biologist spend so much time studying plants? Because she wanted to understand their chlorophylliness.

Why did the chemist want to go to the beach? He wanted to take part in some sodium-chloride reactions!

Why did the microbiologist break up with his girlfriend? They had a breakdown in communication.

Why did the particle physicist team up with a blacksmith? She needed help with her iron nucleus project!

Why is chemistry such a popular sport with scientists? Because there are always plenty of ions to score points with!

How do chemists greet each other during holidays? Happy mole-idays!

How do you know a chemist has been cooking in your kitchen? All the pots and pans are beaker-blackened!

How do you make seven an even number? Take away the 'S'!

What did one atom say to the other atom after an exam? I think I've been split-tested!

What did one DNA molecule say to the other DNA molecule when they bumped into each other? Pardon me, are we related?

After a long work day, what did one DNA strand say to the other? It's been replicating.

What did one gene say to another at recess? Let's get together and double helix around.

What did one gene say to the other gene when they exchanged greetings? It's DNA. Nice to meet you!

What did one geometry book say to the other geometry book? It should be called Plane Interesting!

What did one molecule say to the other after a long journey? It's been a long, hard gas!

What did one neutron say to the other at the

bar? Let's make a subatomic connection!

What did one number say to the other number when they met in a bar? So nice to integer!

What did one proton say to the other after class was canceled? We should just electron away!

What did one protozoan say to another protozoan during lunchtime conversation? Let's make it like amoebas and split!

What did one wave of energy say to the other when they first met? Let's get on the same frequency!

What did the physicist say when he couldn't solve a problem? I need a few more dimensions!

What did the physics professor say to her family during dinner? Such entropy!

What did the snail scientist say when he won the Nobel Prize? I finally got some recognition for my slow and steady research!

What did the thermodynamics professor say when he had a cold? I think I'm feeling some internal energy!

What do you call a cow with two legs? Lean beef!

Why can't mathematicians travel through space? Because there's no answer that's out of this world!

Why did the calculus professor throw a party? He was celebrating derivatives.

Why did the chemist draw a circle on the floor? He wanted to find out where the radius ends!

Why didn't the atom go to school today? Because it lost its electron!

Why do physicists go on dates at 5 pm? Because it's time for some dark-energy romance!

Why do scientists love to go camping? For the fabulous field research!

Why does the sun never set on a physicist's house? Because it's always in motion!

Why don't quantum physicists tell jokes? Because their humor is too atomic!

Why don't scientists do well in court? Because they always object to everything!

Why don't scientists like telling jokes? Because they can never find a punchline.

Why don't astronauts play cards in space? Because they keep floating away!

Why don't astrophysicists gamble? Because they never take any cosmic risks.

Why don't philosophers do well in science class? Because they can never make up their minds!

Why is it so hard for astronauts to pay their bills? They're always orbiting somewhere else!

Why was the calculus teacher so sore after class? She was deriving too much!

Why was the chemist so excited about receiving her degree? She finally graduated from mole-school!

Why was the physics professor so mad after class? He had created too much inertia!

FINALLY, YOU CAN SAY GOOD BYE TO THIS NONSENSE

Whether you're a parent or just someone looking for some lighthearted pun-tastic fun. This is the perfect book to bring out at parties, family reunions, and other gatherings.

Its clever quips and punny one-liners can help break the ice in an uncomfortable situation or give everyone a good laugh after a long day of work.

It's important to remember that dad jokes aren't always appropriate; make sure you know your audience before telling any jokes so as not to offend anyone.

But if used correctly – with timing, simplicity, and context in mind – dad jokes are guaranteed to put smiles on faces!

Dad jokes have been around for many years and have become an increasingly popular form of comedy.

Dad jokes usually feature puns, one-liners, or other types of wordplay, often with the intent of creating a humorous effect.

The origins of dad jokes are somewhat unclear, but they are believed to have originated in the mid-20th century, when fathers began to use puns and other types of jokes to entertain their children.

Dad jokes have since become a popular way for parents to bond with their kids, as well as a way for adults to lighten the mood in any situation.

Nowadays, dad jokes can be found all over the internet, with countless websites and social media accounts dedicated to these kinds of jokes.

Dad jokes are especially popular among Millennials, who often share them on Twitter or other platforms for a quick chuckle.

Q: What did the reader say after finishing a really bad book?

A: Thank goodness I made it through, that was a real page-turner... in the recycle bin!

JACK INK

EPILOGUE

In the waning light, they all stood together and smiled, feeling proud of the long journey they had travelled together.

With one final joke from the dad — something about needing a break now that their adventure was over — they all laughed as they said goodbye and went their separate ways, already planning their next journey together.

AFTERWARD

Afterward, I had a migraine from this book. As time passed, the dad's jokes often aged better than their kids did.

With a wry smile, he'd shake his head and marvel at how the same pun or gag that had once elicited groans and eye rolls from his children now received chuckles and appreciation from adults of all ages.

It was a reminder of the funny — and sometimes dry, sarcastic — journey they'd been on together, one full of laughter and love.

Every now and then, in the middle of a conversation with friends or acquaintances, someone would turn to him and ask if he had any more dad jokes up his sleeve.

He'd respond with a mischievous grin and, if they were lucky, they'd get to hear one of his beloved classics.

Even in their wildest dreams, the kids wouldn't have imagined that one day their father's jokes would be just as beloved by adults as they were by them.

ABOUT THE AUTHOR

Meet Jack "Pun" Ink, a new dad who is spending his time waiting for his son to be born in the hospital.

He has a knack for making puns and using humor to make light of any situation. With years of experience writing jokes and crafting stories, Jack has perfected the art of comedy and loves to bring smiles to those around him.

Whether it's doling out jokes at parties or writing personal biographies like this one, Jack takes pleasure in making others laugh. Just wait until you hear some of the Dad Jokes he's been practicing!

THE BAD DAD JOKE BOOK

PRAISE FOR THE AUTHOR

Jack "Pun" Ink is a true artist of dry humor, sarcasm and wit. His quick-witted comebacks are more than enough to silence any room, and he can craft the perfect joke for any situation.

He's as comfortable taking part in an intellectual conversation as he is making puns at parties - no one ever leaves his presence without being amused!

Jack takes great pleasure in crafting stories that captivate audiences with laughter and delight, proving time and time again that he knows exactly how to bring out the best in humor. –

Penelope "LOL" Puns

ACKNOWLEDGMENTS

Knock-knock?

Who's there?

Dear reader,

I hope you've enjoyed reading my book of dad jokes as much as I enjoyed putting it together.

As a first-time author and probably last-time author, and no publisher would touch this author with a ten-foot pole, I am beyond thrilled that you've taken the time to read my work, and I cannot express enough how grateful I am for your support.

If you've had a good time reading this book and found it to be a source of laughter and joy, I would be humbly asking for your help in spreading the word.

A book review from you, our valued reader, would mean the world to us and would go a long way in helping us reach a wider audience.

So, if you leave us a 5-star review on your favorite platform, it would be an incredible show of support and help us continue to bring joy to others through our love of dad jokes.

Thank you so much for your time and consideration, and I hope you have a pun-tastic day!

Best regards,
Jack "Pun" Ink

SERIOUSLY, I PROMISE.

#THEEND

Made in the USA
Middletown, DE
17 September 2024

60497192R00077